THE WEDDING
PLANNER & RECORD BOOK

Caroline Ash

A DK PUBLISHING BOOK

Design Bernard Higton
Text Caroline Ash

Managing Art Editor Philip Gilderdale
Managing Editor Maureen Rissik
Art Editor Karen Ward
Project Editor Annelise Evans
Production Maryann Rogers
U.S. Editor Laaren Brown

Special photography Guy Ryecart
Border illustration Jane Thomson

First American Edition, 1996
2 4 6 8 10 9 7 5 3

Published in the United States by
DK Publishing, Inc.
95 Madison Avenue, New York, New York 10016

Published in Great Britain by Dorling Kindersley Limited.
Distributed by Houghton Miffin Company, Boston.

ISBN 0-7894-0446-X

Color reproduction by Euroscan in Great Britain
Printed and bound in Singapore by Tien Wah Press

CONTENTS

THE BETROTHAL

Congratulations! Being engaged can be one of the happiest and most romantic times of your life. You have ahead of you all the excitement of planning the wedding, the opportunity to create your perfect day, and the rest of your lives to enjoy being together.

Once you have decided to get married, the first people with whom you will want to share the good news are your parents. It is nice to be able to tell them face to face, perhaps during a meal out, but if this is not practical a telephone call will do. Then tell relatives and close friends, and later work colleagues. Don't be shy about your engagement; most people love to hear good news. A newspaper announcement is a good way of officially informing the world in general.

THE COURTSHIP

WHERE WE MET

WHEN WE MET

HER FIRST IMPRESSION OF HIM

HIS FIRST IMPRESSION OF HER

SPECIAL EVENINGS TOGETHER

THE PROPOSAL

THE SETTING

THE DATE

WHAT HE SAID

YOUR REPLY

THE ENGAGEMENT RING

DESCRIPTION

....

WHY IT WAS CHOSEN

....

WHERE IT WAS PURCHASED

....

CELEBRATIONS

HOW WE CELEBRATED

....

WHAT HER PARENTS SAID

....

WHAT HIS PARENTS SAID

....

Topaz

Turquoise

Garnet

Amethyst

Gemstones and Their Meanings

You might like to choose your birthstone for your engagement ring.

Opal

Aquamarine

Month	Birthstone	Meaning
January	Garnet	Constancy
February	Amethyst	Sincerity
March	Aquamarine	Courage
April	Diamond	Purity
May	Emerald	Success
June	Pearl	Health
July	Ruby	Love
August	Peridot	Happiness
September	Sapphire	Wisdom
October	Opal	Hope
November	Topaz	Faithfulness
December	Turquoise	Harmony

Sapphire

Diamond

Peridot

Emerald

Ruby

Pearl

NEWSPAPER ANNOUNCEMENT

5

PLANNING THE WEDDING

A wedding has great historical and cultural significance and is an important social ritual. It is a rite of passage, the symbolic joining of two people in one of the most venerated partnerships in society. Each wedding is unique, a personal celebration and a highly charged emotional event.

Weddings involve a considerable amount of etiquette and elaborate ritual. They are formal social occasions, steeped in tradition. Breaking away from accepted conventions may confuse your guests, and could even make them feel uncomfortable. Abiding by wedding etiquette helps keep a large gathering of people organized.

Choosing the date

Choose a date when you can both expect to take a reasonable amount of time off from work, both before and after the wedding day. Some dates will be ruled out by personal commitments, for example, exams, job interviews, or professional travel. If either of you suffers from hay fever or any other seasonal illness, avoid the months when it is at its worst. Decide on a time when you will both look and feel your best. Make sure all members of the wedding party are available on the proposed date—your parents, the best man and maid of honor, and also special friends and close relatives.

Once you have agreed upon a suitable date, you should investigate the availability of locations for the ceremony and reception. Check first on the place that is most important to you. If you want to get married in your own church, your first priority should be to make sure that it is free on the proposed date and to reserve it immediately.

Most people choose to have their wedding on a Saturday or Sunday during the summer. Weekends are the most convenient days for guests to attend a wedding, and good weather will contribute to creating that special celebratory atmosphere.

The timing of the wedding ceremony requires some thought. A late morning or early afternoon wedding gives guests enough time to travel to the ceremony and reception, and to return home afterward. If you are not having the ceremony in the same place as the reception, make sure the two sites are reasonably close to each other; guests who have already traveled some distance to get to the wedding will not relish a long journey to the reception.

> When I was a young man I vowed never to marry until I found the ideal woman. Well, I found her—but, alas, she was waiting for the ideal man.
>
> ROBERT SCHUMANN (GERMAN COMPOSER)

Members of the Wedding Party

Asking a friend to fulfill an important role at your wedding is a heartfelt way of acknowledging how much you value your friendship. Use the space below to record the names of your attendants and the members of the wedding party, and the reasons why you chose them.

....

MOTHER OF THE BRIDE
....

FATHER OF THE BRIDE
....

MOTHER OF THE GROOM
....

FATHER OF THE GROOM
....

THE BEST MAN
CHOSEN BECAUSE
....

MAID OF HONOR
CHOSEN BECAUSE
....

BRIDESMAID
CHOSEN BECAUSE
....

BRIDESMAID
CHOSEN BECAUSE
....

BRIDESMAID
CHOSEN BECAUSE
....

FLOWER GIRL
CHOSEN BECAUSE
....

USHERS
CHOSEN BECAUSE
....

....

The Legal Requirements

Before you can get married, you need a marriage license. Call city hall in your town or the county clerk to determine the legal requirements in your area and if you need an appointment to get a license. Both the bride and the groom must go to the office to apply, and both must wait while the application is processed. A fee is charged for preparing the license. You will need to bring certain papers with you, usually proof of citizenship, proof of age, the results of your blood tests, and proof of divorce (if applicable). There may be more requirements if either the bride or the groom is under 18.

Depending on the state, the license is valid for 30 or 60 days; if you do not get married before the license expires, you must get a new license. A waiting period (often 24 to 72 hours) also applies—you cannot get the license and get married on the same day.

Getting a license can be fun. Yes, you are dealing with a government bureaucracy—but the atmosphere at city hall may be quite festive. If you are getting your license in a big city, you will meet other couples applying for licenses; if you live in a small town, the office workers may make a fuss over you. Like so many other events surrounding your wedding, this is a once-in-a-lifetime experience. Enjoy it!

TYPES OF CEREMONY

Most Judeo-Christian and civil ceremonies have the same basic structure: the couple comes in, is given in marriage, exchanges vows and rings, is pronounced husband and wife, and exits. (The kiss is optional.) It's up to you to take this framework and build your ceremony as you will build your marriage.

Civil ceremony

A town official, justice of the peace, or judge will officiate at a civil ceremony, which may be held at city hall or in the judge's chambers—or anywhere the official will travel. (Contact the county clerk's office or city for specifics.)

A civil ceremony involves a convocation and the vows, and then the official pronounces you husband and wife. If you have specific concerns, be sure to ask the official exactly what he or she will say *before* the ceremony—some do mention God or pronounce the couple man and wife. Officials frequently add a personal stamp in the form of a poem or quotation, although they will usually be happy to read any brief item you supply.

Remember that if you get married in a public building, the size of the room many limit the number of guests who can attend the ceremony. If this is the case, you will have to restrict invitations to the ceremony to family and close friends, but you can ask a larger number of guests to the reception.

Protestant

Protestant weddings are performed by a minister or other official of the church. Most ceremonies are flexible enough to accommodate special readings or hymns during the course of the service. In most ceremonies, the minister blesses the couple. He or she will then ask who gives the bride in marriage, and who gives the groom; this is usually their respective parents.

Now is the time for the vows. The minister says to the bride, "Will you have this man to be your husband; to live together in the covenant of marriage? Will you love him, comfort him, honor and keep him, in sickness and in health, and, forsaking all others, be faithful to him as long as you both shall live?" The bride answers. The groom is asked the same question and answers. The groom then takes the bride's right hand and makes his vows: "I, (his name), take you, (her name), to be my wife, to have and to hold from this day forward, for better or for worse, for richer, for poorer, in sickness and in health, to love and to cherish, until death do we part." The couple then exchange rings, and the minister pronounces them husband and wife, concluding, "Those whom God has joined, let no man put asunder." The newlyweds may kiss. A final prayer is made.

Different denominations have different versions of this basic ceremony. Consult with your minister to get specific details.

Roman Catholic

At the ceremony, the priest makes an introductory prayer, then asks the man and woman individually if they have come "freely and without reservation to give yourselves to each other in marriage."

The bride and the groom join hands, and the groom says, "I, (his name), take you, (her name), to be my wife..." making his vows to love and protect his new wife throughout life. The bride makes similar vows. The priest blesses them and then the rings. The groom places the ring on

True it is that marriages be done in heaven and performed on earth.

WILLIAM PAINTER, *PALACE OF PLEASURE*

the bride's ring finger, saying, "(Her name), take this ring as a sign of my love and faithfulness. In the name of the Father, and of the Son, and of the Holy Spirit." The bride puts the ring on the groom's ring finger with the same words. The priest makes a nuptial blessing and concludes the ceremony. Often, the newlyweds kiss before beginning the recessional. The ceremony is part of a nuptial mass. Again, different parishes have different versions of the wedding ceremony; consult with your priest for specifics.

Jewish

The couple and the rabbi gather under the *chuppah* (wedding canopy). Their rabbi blesses the couple with the *birchot erusin* (betrothal blessings), said over a cup of wine. The bride and groom sip from the cup. Two witnesses are called up. Then the groom places the ring (a plain band) on the bride's forefinger and says, "Behold, you are consecrated unto me by this ring, according to the law of Moses and of Israel." Now the bride and groom are wedded. (Practice this sentence in Hebrew and English—the rabbi will prompt you, but it's easy to make mistakes when you are nervous.) The rabbi or a guest will read the *ketubah* (marriage contract). If it is a double-ring ceremony, the bride gives the groom his ring. Then the rabbi or seven different guests will make seven blessings (the *birchot nissuin*) over another cup of wine. The bride and groom drink from the cup. Symbolically, the groom breaks a glass by stepping on it; the guests cheer and shout "*Mazel tov*," and the bride and groom kiss. Reform, Conservative, and Orthodox groups have different rituals; consult with your rabbi for specifics.

Quaker

Quaker ceremonies require approval from the monthly meeting under whose care you will be married. They usually take place during a Quaker meeting called for the purpose. Friends and guests worship. The couple enters (in a procession if desired) and joins the meeting. After a silence, the bride and groom stand up, joining hands. The groom says his vows, then the bride says hers. Another person pronounces them married. The wedding certificate (usually read aloud) is brought to the couple to sign, and then the guests sign. The traditional ceremony does not involve rings, a bridal party, or giving the bride away. The Quaker ceremony may be structured as the bridal couple wishes, as long as the wedding remains simple.

Other ceremonies

There are as many wedding ceremonies as there are couples who wish to wed. Just as every couple is unique, every wedding ceremony is unique. Work with each other to create a wedding ceremony that is yours alone.

PLANNING THE RECEPTION

The key to a successful reception is to plan ahead, paying attention to detail, and to give careful thought to your guests' needs and preferences so that they all have a wonderful time that they will remember for years to come.

Choosing the reception hall
The choice of sites is enormous, ranging from a hotel or reception rooms with catering provided, to a hall or rooms with no caterers, to a tent set up on your parents' lawn. You need to be confident that the basic requirements for entertaining a large number of people, such as catering, cloakroom facilities, bathrooms, and parking, can all be adequately provided. A hotel can meet these needs, and its staff is experienced in running wedding receptions and ironing out any minor hitches that may arise. Hotels are likely to be expensive, however, and the atmosphere can often seem impersonal. Spacious, ornate rooms or beautiful gardens with or without caterers can make an unusual and delightful setting for the reception.

If you have the space, and the time of year is right, a tent on your lawn or at your parents' home has many advantages. For a summer wedding, a tent provides an attractive outdoor setting and the benefit of shelter in case of rain. The relaxed atmosphere of the family home will put guests at their ease, although there may be inconveniences such as limited parking. It is also a cost-effective option, and you retain control over the choice of caterers and other services used.

The wedding banquet
It is advisable to have a sit-down meal after the wedding ceremony, if space permits, as many of your guests will have traveled for some distance and may be tired, and older relations and friends will appreciate being able to sit down. Whether you are giving a light buffet or a grand formal banquet, seat guests according to a seating plan (see pages 52—53). You can either have servers bringing the food to your guests at their tables, or a buffet, in which guests go up to the serving table and help themselves.

Caterers
Some people like to provide the catering for the wedding themselves, but unless the guest list is exceptionally small, this can be quite an undertaking. Most people opt for employing caterers. Some places, such as hotels, stipulate that in-house caterers must be used, while others will leave the choice up to you. Examine the caterers' menus, ask to sample the food, and meet with the catering manager in person to discuss your requirements. Have a fairly firm idea of how many guests you will have and, working with the manager, determine the staff you will need, choose the menu, list in detail any equipment and linen you wish to use, and confirm whether or not the caterers are responsible for cleaning up afterward. Make sure you have all the relevant information in writing.

Food
When deciding on the menu, remember that you will be catering to a variety of different ages and tastes. It is not a good idea to attempt to serve anything too controversial; stick to dependable classics. Hot food is difficult to serve simultaneously to a large number of people, and to do so requires adequate catering facilities and staff. Provision should be made for any special dietary requirements of your guests; remember to include at least one dish that is appropriate for vegetarians. If you are inviting children, try to include food that will appeal to them. Your caterer will probably have more suggestions and specialties than you ever thought possible.

Drinks

Drinks should be served to your guests as soon they arrive at the reception— wine, champagne, and sparkling wine are popular favorites. For the cocktail hour and in many cases during the meal, many people will enjoy mixed drinks and spirits. When choosing wine to be served with the meal, make sure that it complements the food. A light, fresh wine is an ideal choice at lunchtime in the summer. Offer people red or white wine and a comprehensive selection of nonalcoholic drinks for drivers, nondrinkers, and children. It is a thoughtful gesture to offer beer for those who prefer it to wine. Champagne or sparkling wine would be a suitably festive drink for the toasts, if finances allow. If the reception is being held at a hotel or restaurant, you may find that they insist on supplying all the drinks. This can be a very expensive option and should be taken into consideration when choosing and pricing the reception site. Other places may allow you to bring your own alcohol and soft drinks, but will charge a corkage fee for serving it. Calculate the quantity of drinks you are likely to need, using the guide at left, but remember that these are approximate measures. Many people drink quite a bit at weddings, so make sure that you have ample supplies.

Drink Allowances

	Glasses per guest	per bottle
Cocktail hour		
Wine	1 – 2	6 – 8
Spirits	1 – 2	30
Mixers w/spirits	1 – 2	5
During meal		
Wine	3 – 4	6 – 8
Toasts		
Champagne	1 – 2	6 – 8
Liqueurs	1 – 2	1 quart = 25 drinks
Soft drinks		Allow between half a quart and a quart per guest

The cake

The cake is an important focal point of the reception; it may even be on display throughout the celebrations. First decide on the style of cake, how many tiers you would like, and what sort of cake and filling you would like. Choose a baker who is experienced and skilled in decorating wedding cakes: these baked behemoths can be incredibly beautiful and intricate. The cake should be large enough for all your guests to have a piece. Many couples like to save the top tier of the cake to celebrate their first wedding anniversary, it should be frozen until then.

Entertainment

Should both space and budget allow, musicians or singers performing at your wedding help create a festive atmosphere. Ask friends for recommendations and listen to demo tapes. Whether you choose an eight-piece orchestra with a singer, a disc jockey with hundreds of records, or a string quartet, make sure the musicians can play the songs that are important to you. These may include your first dance, your parents' wedding songs, favorite numbers in dance arrangements, standards, and ethnic specialties. Younger guests will be delighted if you have hired an entertainer or magician to amuse them, as children are frequently overlooked at weddings. Book any entertainment as early as possible to be certain of getting your first choice.

WEDDING CHECKLIST

Organizing a wedding is complicated, and it is important to select and reserve the ceremony and reception sites as early as possible. Once you have drawn up a master plan, the project will seem less daunting, and you can devote yourself to the planning of every detail. Follow a timetable to make sure that nothing is forgotten. In the countdown to the wedding, you can check the list each week, and see what needs to be done and who needs to be contacted, so your wedding day will be enjoyed and remembered by everyone.

Nine to Three Months Ahead

CHOOSE ATTENDANTS:

MAID OF HONOR

BRIDESMAIDS

BEST MAN

USHERS

RESERVE CEREMONY SITE

RESERVE RECEPTION SITE

RESERVE HOTEL FOR WEDDING NIGHT

SELECT MUSICIANS

MAKE HONEYMOON ARRANGEMENTS

SELECT CATERERS

SELECT FLORIST

Six to Three Months Ahead

CHOOSE AND ORDER WEDDING OUTFITS:

FOR BRIDE

FOR GROOM

FOR ATTENDANTS

PLAN CEREMONY

CHOOSE MUSIC AND SERVICE

DRAW UP GUEST LIST

PLAN AND PRINT INVITATIONS AND OTHER STATIONERY

SELECT PHOTOGRAPHER/VIDEOGRAPHER

ORDER WEDDING CAKE

ARRANGE MARRIAGE LICENSE

CHOOSE WEDDING RINGS

DRAW UP WEDDING PRESENT LIST

RESERVE TRANSPORTATION TO CEREMONY AND RECEPTION

RESERVE OVERNIGHT ACCOMMODATIONS FOR GUESTS

ARRANGE PARKING FOR GUESTS

ARRANGE PASSPORTS/VISAS/VACCINATIONS FOR HONEYMOON

Twelve to Six Weeks Ahead

SEND OUT INVITATIONS

RESERVE HAIRDRESSER

RESERVE MAKEUP ARTIST

DISCUSS MENU WITH CATERERS

DISCUSS FLOWERS WITH FLORIST

ARRANGE WEDDING REHEARSAL AND DINNER

BUY THANK-YOU GIFTS FOR ATTENDANTS

Three to Two Weeks Ahead

SEND WEDDING ANNOUNCEMENT TO THE NEWSPAPER

DRAW UP SEATING PLAN FOR RECEPTION

CHECK CEREMONY AND LEGAL ARRANGEMENTS

CONFIRM RECEPTION SITE

CONFIRM PARKING FOR GUESTS

CONFIRM OVERNIGHT ACCOMMODATIONS FOR GUESTS

CONFIRM CATERERS AND FINALIZE NUMBER OF GUESTS

CONFIRM BAR ARRANGEMENTS

ORDER DRINKS

CONFIRM FLORIST

CONFIRM PHOTOGRAPHER/VIDEOGRAPHER

CHECK AND TRY ON FULL BRIDAL OUTFIT

PRACTICE MAKEUP AND HAIR

SCHEDULE FINAL FITTING FOR DRESS

CONFIRM GROOM'S OUTFIT

CONFIRM ATTENDANTS' OUTFITS

CONFIRM HONEYMOON ARRANGEMENTS

CHECK HONEYMOON WARDROBE

ARRANGE BRIDESMAIDS' PARTY

PACK FOR HONEYMOON

One Week Ahead

DOUBLE-CHECK ALL ARRANGEMENTS

INVITING THE GUESTS

INVITATION

A wedding is a formal social occasion, and invitations usually conform to a strict code of etiquette in their wording. They are traditionally sent from the hosts of the wedding reception, and written in the third person. The invitation should include the following information: the names of the people who are hosting the celebrations, the names of the bride and groom, the date, time, and location of the ceremony and the reception, and details of where to send the reply. Many people include a printed reply card. If children are being invited, this can be made clear by including their names on the invitation to their parents. Anyone over the age of eighteen should be sent a separate invitation. If you would like to give a single friend the option of bringing a partner or friend, add "and guest" after their name on the invitation. Include with the invitation any maps

EXAMPLES OF WORDINGS FOR INVITATIONS

The bride's parents as hosts:
(ceremony in a house of worship)

Mr. and Mrs. Timothy Mitchell
request the honor of
your presence
at the marriage
of their daughter
Anne
to
Mr. Jeremy Barden
on Saturday, the third of June,
at two o'clock
First Community Church
Milltown, New Jersey

---

*Invitation to the reception only, if
hosted by the bride's parents:*

Mr. and Mrs. Timothy Mitchell
request the pleasure of
your company at a reception
following the marriage
of their daughter
Anne
to
Mr. Jeremy Barden
at Fairwinds Country Club
Milltown, New Jersey
on Saturday, the third of June,
at four o'clock

---

*The bride's parents are divorced,
but are hosting the reception jointly:*

Mr. Timothy Mitchell and
Mrs. Claire Edwards
request the honor of
your presence
at the marriage
of their daughter
Anne
to
Mr. Jeremy Barden
on Saturday, the third of June,
at two o'clock
First Community Church
Milltown, New Jersey

---

*The bride and groom are hosting the
wedding and reception:*
(ceremony at home or in a hotel or hall)

The pleasure of your company
is requested at the wedding of
Anne Mitchell
and
Jeremy Barden
on Saturday, the third of June,
at two o'clock
Fairwinds Country Club
Milltown, New Jersey

R.s.v.p.
95 Sutherland Avenue
Binghamton, New York

---

and directions that the guests will need to travel to the ceremony and reception, and make sure that parking places at both sites are clearly indicated. If necessary, send information on accommodations with the invitation.

If you are having the invitations printed, the process can take several weeks from start to finish, so give yourself enough time to fit it comfortably into your schedule. Send invitations out 8 to 12 weeks before the actual wedding date to give your guests adequate notice. Traditionally, invitations to formal weddings were hand engraved in copperplate, a process which is very expensive and takes a long time. Thermographic printing gives the same raised typeface at a considerably lower price, and

so is a more popular option for slightly less formal weddings. For an informal invitation, you can choose any color ink and any typeface, and you may include a decorative border, photograph, or drawing. Whichever method of printing or style of invitation you choose, check the typesetting carefully to make sure it is absolutely correct, and ask for more invitations than you actually need. Now is the time to order any other wedding stationery you may require; for example, menu cards, place cards, bridal stationery, thank-you notes, napkins, or matchbooks.

THE GUEST LIST

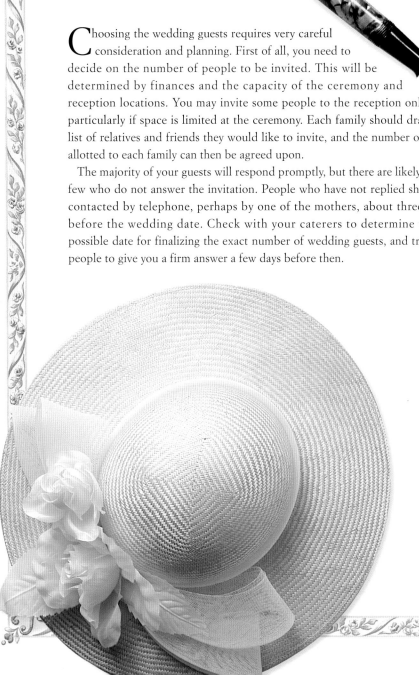

Choosing the wedding guests requires very careful consideration and planning. First of all, you need to decide on the number of people to be invited. This will be determined by finances and the capacity of the ceremony and reception locations. You may invite some people to the reception only, particularly if space is limited at the ceremony. Each family should draw up a list of relatives and friends they would like to invite, and the number of guests allotted to each family can then be agreed upon.

The majority of your guests will respond promptly, but there are likely to be a few who do not answer the invitation. People who have not replied should be contacted by telephone, perhaps by one of the mothers, about three weeks before the wedding date. Check with your caterers to determine the last possible date for finalizing the exact number of wedding guests, and try to get people to give you a firm answer a few days before then.

NAME   REPLY RECEIVED

....

....

....

....

....

....

....

....

....

....

....

....

....

....

....

NAME	REPLY RECEIVED	NAME	REPLY RECEIVED

NAME   REPLY RECEIVED   NAME   REPLY RECEIVED

....

....

....

....

....

....

....

....

....

....

....

....

....

....

....

....

NAME	REPLY RECEIVED	NAME	REPLY RECEIVED
....	....	....	....
....	....	....	....
....	....	....	....
....	....	....	....
....	....	....	....
....	....	....	....
....	....	....	....
....	....	....	....
....	....	....	....
....	....	....	....
....	....	....	....
....	....	....	....
....	....	....	....

NAME

REPLY RECEIVED

NAME

REPLY RECEIVED

ACCOMMODATIONS FOR GUESTS

Guests traveling some distance to your wedding will need help in finding accommodations for the night after, and in some cases the night before, the wedding. Make a list of hotels in the area, with a brief description of each one, including a price guideline and distance from the wedding, and send it to any guests who may need it. If you have a large number of people who require accommodations, you may be able to negotiate a special rate at a nearby hotel. Keep a record of who is staying where, so that out-of-town guests and important people can be contacted easily.

NAME OF GUEST(S)

HOTEL NAME

ADDRESS

ROOM NUMBER

TELEPHONE NUMBER

DATE OF ARRIVAL

NUMBER OF NIGHTS OF STAY

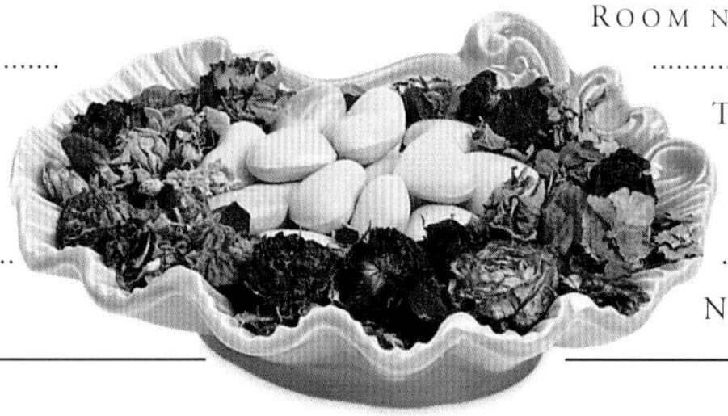

NAME OF GUEST(S)

HOTEL NAME

ADDRESS

ROOM NUMBER

TELEPHONE NUMBER

DATE OF ARRIVAL

NUMBER OF NIGHTS OF STAY

NAME OF GUEST(S)

HOTEL NAME

ADDRESS

ROOM NUMBER

TELEPHONE NUMBER

DATE OF ARRIVAL

NUMBER OF NIGHTS OF STAY

NAME OF GUEST(S)

HOTEL NAME

ADDRESS

ROOM NUMBER

TELEPHONE NUMBER

DATE OF ARRIVAL

NUMBER OF NIGHTS OF STAY

THE WEDDING LIST

Once the invitations have been sent out, the wedding list can be drawn up. A list is a practical and acceptable way of letting your guests know which gifts you would like. Many of your guests will appreciate your suggestions. It is traditional to ask for items for the home, which both of you can use and enjoy, as opposed to something personal. Set aside a reasonable amount of time so that you can make the list together—it is a task that should be fun to do. The list can be as diverse as you like; in fact, it is tactful and courteous to include a wide variety of objects in a range of prices, so that each guest can find something they would like to give you that is also within their budget.

You can compile your own list, or register with a large store or your favorite specialty store. Most large nationwide department stores offer a bridal registry, and will supply a form for you to fill in with your individual requirements. This list is then entered into the store's computer system, with gifts organized by department and price. Guests may visit their area store in person to choose a present, or they can order one by telephone. The store records what each guest has purchased and constantly updates the computerized list to avoid duplication. Many mail-order companies that specialize in china and flatware also offer a bridal registry. Even if you register with a department store, you can still have an independent list as well, because some guests may not want to use the store, and will ask for alternative suggestions.

It is usual for the bride's mother to oversee the wedding list. Guests contact her, and she can either give details about the bridal registry or send a copy of the list. If you have compiled your own list, she will need to confirm who is buying what, and cross off each suggestion once the gift has been purchased.

Whatever system you choose, be sure to divide the wedding list into general sections such as flatware, china, glass, cutlery, kitchenware, linen, and so forth. Be as specific as possible about the brand, style, color, and number of items required. This makes it easy to stay organized.

OUR WEDDING LIST IS HELD AT

ITEM	AVAILABLE FROM	PRICE	ITEM	AVAILABLE FROM	PRICE

ITEM	AVAILABLE FROM	PRICE

ITEM	AVAILABLE FROM	PRICE

ITEM	AVAILABLE FROM	PRICE

ITEM	AVAILABLE FROM	PRICE

ITEM	AVAILABLE FROM	PRICE

ITEM	AVAILABLE FROM	PRICE

CHOOSING THE PHOTOGRAPHER

The best way to find a photographer is by personal recommendation; failing that, you will have to resort to scouring local directories. It is advisable to select and reserve a photographer at least three months before the wedding date. Visit any photographers you think might be suitable and ask to see examples of their work. If the firm is a large one, make sure that you look at the work of an individual photographer and book him for your wedding. Check if a backup photographer is provided if he falls ill on the day.

The composition of the photographs should be planned and agreed upon with the photographer in advance. Decide in precise detail what you would like to be photographed, specify whether you want glossy or matt prints and the size of prints you would like, and confirm everything in writing. Give the photographer a comprehensive timetable of the whole day.

Comparing the cost of different photographers can be confusing. Some offer a wedding package that includes an agreed number of prints given to you in an album, while others charge a flat hourly rate, and some charge only for prints. The wedding package can be cost-effective, but if the photographer chooses the prints, it means you risk being presented with photographs you do not like. If an hourly rate is offered, ask how much you will be charged for prints, and agree on how long the photographer will stay. The photographer usually retains the copyright and the negatives of the photographs, but you may be able to negotiate a deal whereby the negatives revert to you after six months.

Professional photographers are expensive, but you could cut the cost by employing a professional to record the ceremony and take formal photographs immediately afterwards, and then relying on friends and family to cover the reception. Ask several people to take informal photographs, so the responsibility does not rest on one individual. Shots of your guests enjoying themselves make delightful mementos. Be courteous and ask for permission from the minister or registrar if you want the ceremony photographed. Some places ban the use of flashes, but are happy to accommodate other photography.

Choosing the videographer

Recording the highlights of the wedding day on video is a practical way to preserve your memories. It is also a wonderful way to share the day with people who have been unable to attend the wedding due to ill-health or difficulties with travel. Ask a competent friend or relative to video the day's events, or employ a professional. Follow the same procedure to that used in choosing a photographer. Ask the videographer how obtrusive he will be, particularly if he plans to use special lighting equipment. Check that the original video can be copied easily, and remember that the videographer retains the copyright, so you may not be able to keep the master tape, which will have the best quality picture. Ask your official whether it is permissible to videotape the ceremony.

THE BRIDAL CARRIAGE

Arriving at the ceremony in a fairy-tale horse-drawn carriage, a white limousine, or a vintage Rolls Royce or Bentley fulfills many brides' fantasies. Alternative modes of transportation include a classic car, a black or white London taxi, a sedan chair, or a friend's sports car decorated with ribbons. You're limited only by your imagination.

Should you decide to rent a car, you will find that most limousine companies charge an hourly rate that includes the services of a chauffeur and virtually unlimited mileage. Give yourself ample time if you are reserving a car at an hourly rate. Some companies charge a flat fee for a wedding, giving you use of the car for a specified amount of time. The limousine will take you to the ceremony, wait for you outside, and then take you and the groom to the reception. Send a map showing the location of the ceremony and reception and details of the estimated timetable to the limousine company, to avoid confusion. If your dress has full skirts, check that there will be enough room inside the car to avoid getting it crushed, and be sure you can get out of the car easily and gracefully when you arrive at the ceremony.

Practical considerations can be swept aside in deciding what form of transportation will take you from the reception, especially if money is no object

on this special day. You can be whisked away by helicopter, light airplane, hot-air balloon, rowboat, motorboat, gondola, motorcycle, tandem, pony and trap, or on horseback. The possibilities are endless.

Transportation to the ceremony should be arranged for the wedding party to arrive before the bride. The groom and best man should leave first in one car, then the bride's mother (if she is not in the bridal car) and the bridesmaids in another. The groom's parents and any grandparents may require another car:

Bridal Car	Car Number Two	Car Number Three
Bride	Best man	Mother of the bride
Father of the bride	Groom	(in traditonal
(and mother of the bride		etiquette)
in modern etiquette)		Bridesmaids

Marriage is the life-long miracle,
The self-begetting wonder, daily fresh.

CHARLES KINGSLEY, *THE SAINT'S TRAGEDY*

Daisy, Daisy, give me your answer, do!
I'm half crazy, all for the love of you!
It won't be a stylish marriage,
I can't afford a carriage,
But you'll look sweet upon the seat
Of a bicycle made for two!

HARRY DACRE, *DAISY BELL*

$\mathcal{F}$LOWERS

Flowers play a special part in a wedding, contributing to the sense of celebration and occasion. Chosen with care, flowers can add a marvelous sense of beauty to the ceremony and reception, and they give the finishing touches to the outfits of the bride, groom, and attendants.

When choosing a florist, ask to see photographs and examples of their work. Make sure that the florist will be able to supply all the flowers and foliage on the actual day of the wedding. Choose flowers that will be in season and readily available, particularly if substantial quantities will be needed.

If you have decided on a color scheme for the wedding, choose flowers that are in keeping with it. Pink, blue, purple, yellow, and white flowers are the most popular choices. Blue and yellow flowers are pretty and fresh for a spring wedding; hazy purples and pinks are reflective of midsummer; and for a winter or autumn wedding russets, reds, and oranges are effective.

Flowers for the wedding party
Flowers are a traditional part of a bride's outfit. Most brides carry a bouquet, which can range from a simple arrangement of country flowers to a wired bridal shower. Flowers for the bouquet can be chosen because they are particular favorites and also for their symbolic value. Headdresses can be enhanced with the addition of a few fresh sprigs of flowers, especially if the bride wears her hair long and flowing.

Bridesmaids can carry small bouquets, or decorated hoops or baskets of flowers. Simple circlets made out of flowers look charming on little girls. The mothers (and grandmothers) of the bride and groom traditionally wear a corsage, usually a spray of flowers chosen to suit their individual outfits. The rest of the wedding party, including the groom, usually wear boutonnieres—a single flower offset by foliage, reflecting the wedding color scheme.

The Language of Flowers

Camellia	Gratitude
Carnation	Pure love
Daisy	Sharing
Forget-me-not	Remembrance
Honeysuckle	Fidelity
Iris	Health
Lily	Purity
Lily of the valley	Happiness
Phlox	Togetherness
Rose	Virtue and beauty
Violet	Faithfulness

Flowers for the Wedding Party

THE BRIDE

FLOWERS IN BOUQUET

DESCRIPTION OF SHAPE AND STYLE

FLOWERS IN HAIR

BRIDE'S ATTENDANTS

BRIDESMAIDS' FLOWERS

BRIDESMAIDS' HEADDRESSES

FLOWER GIRLS' CIRCLETS AND PETALS

THE GROOM AND GROOMSMEN

GROOM: DESCRIPTION OF BOUTONNIERE

BEST MAN AND USHERS: DESCRIPTION OF BOUTONNIERES

THE MOTHERS

MOTHER OF THE BRIDE: DESCRIPTION OF CORSAGE

MOTHER OF THE GROOM: DESCRIPTION OF CORSAGE

FLOWERS FOR THE CEREMONY AND RECEPTION

A spartan reception hall, the blank sides of a tent, or the austere stonework of a church can be transformed instantly with a few strategically placed flower arrangements. Skillful use of foliage and flowers can conceal unattractive elements and accentuate charming features to give your wedding a special, celebratory atmosphere.

For maximum impact, place flowers for the ceremony near the place where the bride and groom will make their vows. In a church, floral arrangements on either side of the altar are customary. Remember that many guests will be seated some distance away from the altar, so these arrangements must be large and imposing. Large rooms, especially sanctuaries in places of worship, are not always particularly well illuminated, so use either very pale or vividly colored flowers and foliage to make sure they are clearly visible.

At the reception hall, large expanses of empty wall can be used as a stunning backdrop for dramatic flower arrangements.

Flowers for the Ceremony

These can be placed on small tables or pedestals covered in pretty fabric. Garlands look very beautiful wrapped around poles or pillars, or hung in swags across a wall or entrance.

Floral displays can be prohibitively expensive, not least because they require hours of work to assemble. You could reduce the cost by asking a friend or relative who has experience with flowers to create some of the arrangements for you. Table centerpieces are reasonably easy to make using carnations, ferns, and gypsophila held securely in place with florist's oasis. For a spring wedding, you could plant or buy little pots of dwarf bulbs to use as table centerpieces—keep an eye on them to make sure they will be in bloom on the wedding day—and decorate them with moss and foliage. Plunder your garden for ivy or greenery; use large quantities to drape around a room or decorate the front of a covered table. (Greenery dries out quickly, so soak the cut ends in water for 48 hours before using.)

Flowers for the Reception

IN THE ENTRANCES

ON THE HEAD TABLE

BY THE RECEIVING LINE

In Eastern lands they talk in flowers,
And they tell in a garland their loves and cares;
Each blossom that blooms in their garden bowers,
On its leaves a mystic language bears.

JAMES GATES PERCIVAL, *THE LANGUAGE OF FLOWERS*

TABLE CENTERPIECE

BESIDE THE CAKE

"THROWING BOUQUET"

FLOWERS AS MEMENTOS

Preserving some of the flowers from your wedding day is a wonderful way of remembering their beauty in years to come. You could save and press some of the flowers from your bridal bouquet or headdress, from the bouquets of your attendants, and from the arrangements at the ceremony and reception. Press the flowers between clean paper with heavy weights for about two months to allow them to dry out completely.

Flowers from the Bridal Bouquet

In emerald tufts, flowers purple, blue and white;
Like sapphire, pearl and rich embroidery.

WILLIAM SHAKESPEARE, *THE MERRY WIVES OF WINDSOR*

THE WEDDING CLOTHES

THE BRIDAL GOWN

You will remember your wedding dress all your life, and it should be the most beautiful dress you will ever wear. You are free to indulge your fantasies because you will be the focus of attention throughout the celebrations. Choose a shape that flatters you, in which you feel comfortable but elegant. Resist the temptation to order a dress that is too small in the hope that you will lose weight. If you do not manage to diet successfully, the dress will feel tight and will not look as nice. Some brides find that with all the excitement they do lose a few pounds, so a final fitting a week or two before the wedding is advisable. Many brides choose their dress in the belief that they will have it altered and wear it afterward, but very few ever do. It is a special dress for a special day, and there is no point in compromising.

Bridal magazines are rich catalogs of wedding dresses and can help you choose your favorite style before you shop. If you are looking for classic style, historical fashion books are a good source of inspiration. A 19th-century or early 20th-century evening dress could be copied by a dressmaker. The formality of the wedding will influence the length of the train; the longest, cathedral length, is the most formal. Choose a color that suits your complexion: off-white flatters pale complexions, while bright white complements darker skin. Pale pastels from pearl gray to pink can be becoming.

Consider what the temperature may be on the wedding day—you do not want to end up overheated or shivering. Layers of long petticoats or a tight bodice could make you swelter uncomfortably in the summer, and you may need a wrap or jacket, in a suitable coordinating fabric, for a chilly autumn day.

STYLE

TYPE OF FABRIC

AMOUNT OF FABRIC USED

MEASUREMENTS:

BUST

WAIST

LENGTH OF SKIRT

LENGTH OF TRAIN

WHERE THE DRESS WAS MADE OR PURCHASED

DATE OF FIRST FITTING

DATE OF SECOND FITTING

DATE OF FINAL FITTING

There is something about a wedding gown prettier than any other gown in the world.

DOUGLAS JERROLD, *A WEDDING GOWN*

PHOTOGRAPH OF THE
BRIDAL GOWN

SWATCH OF FABRIC FROM
THE BRIDAL GOWN

BRIDAL ACCESSORIES

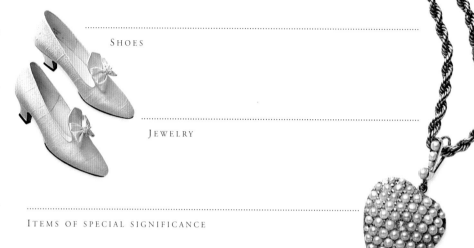

Once you have decided on the dress, you can turn your attention to the rest of the outfit. A headdress and veil are traditionally worn with a long bridal gown. In earlier times, the wedding couple were covered by translucent material to shield their faces from the multitude. Today, the veil preserves the modesty of the bride. You will probably want to remove the veil after the ceremony, so be sure the headdress looks good on its own. Bridal slippers can be delicately embroidered or dyed to match the dress precisely—or even made of the same fabric as the dress.

Keep jewelry as simple as possible so that it does not detract from either the dress or your bridal radiance. A single string of pearls and plain earrings are flattering and stylish. Family heirlooms that have personal significance—for example, your grandmother's favorite brooch or the pearls your mother wore on her wedding day—can add a special touch. According to the well-known adage, it is customary to wear:

> Something old,
> Something new,
> Something borrowed,
> Something blue.
>
> ANON

SHOES

....

JEWELRY

....

ITEMS OF SPECIAL SIGNIFICANCE

....

VEIL

....

HEADDRESS

....

BRIDE'S ATTENDANTS

As you decide on the outfits for the bridesmaids and attendants, there are a variety of considerations. First, the dresses should harmonize with the bride's outfit. Second, the colors chosen should reflect the color themes of the wedding. Third, the color selected should suit the complexion of each attendant, and the dresses should be in a style that all the bridesmaids find flattering and comfortable to wear.

MAID OR MATRON OF HONOR'S OUTFIT
....

DRESS

....

SHOES

....

ACCESSORIES

....

BRIDESMAIDS' OUTFITS
....

DRESSES

....

SHOES

....

ACCESSORIES

....

PHOTOGRAPH
OR
SWATCH OF FABRIC FROM
BRIDESMAIDS' DRESSES

....

OUTFITS OF RINGBEARER AND FLOWER GIRLS

....

GIFTS FROM BRIDE

....

THE GROOM'S OUTFIT

Most grooms wear a suit for the wedding, either purchased or rented for the occasion. The type of suit he wears will depend on the time of day and style of the wedding. Strictly speaking, morning dress is not worn in the evening or late afternoon, and it is the traditional option for a formal affair. If the wedding is taking place later in the day, the groom may want to wear black tie. He could also wear a well-cut dark business suit. If the groom is in the armed forces, he may want to wear his dress uniform. The groomsmen and male family members should follow the groom's lead.

GROOM'S OUTFIT

....

SUIT

....

SHIRT

....

TIE

....

SHOES

....

ACCESSORIES

....

PHOTOGRAPH OF GROOM
AND BEST MAN

BEST MAN AND USHERS

....

DESCRIPTION OF OUTFITS

....

MOTHERS OF THE BRIDE AND GROOM

PHOTOGRAPH OF THE MOTHERS
OF THE BRIDE AND GROOM

The mother of the bride plays a key role in the celebrations, and many eyes will be on her. It is advisable for her to wear an outfit that is stylish but comfortable, as weddings can be physically strenuous for the hosts, involving a great deal of hand-shaking and running around taking care of guests. A tailored suit or an elegant dress, perhaps with a hat, would be appropriate. The two mothers need to work together to make sure that their outfits are complementary and in keeping with the colors chosen by the bride.

MOTHER OF THE BRIDE'S OUTFIT

DRESS/SUIT

ACCESSORIES

MOTHER OF THE GROOM'S OUTFIT

DRESS/SUIT

ACCESSORIES

PREWEDDING CELEBRATIONS

Traditionally the bride and groom celebrate their final days as single people with bachelor and bachelorette parties, which are exclusively all-male and all-female affairs respectively.

Bachelor parties can be held in a bar, a restaurant or a club. They used to be held on the night before the wedding, but now more usually occur during the week before the wedding day, to give the groom time to recover. The best man is responsible for organizing the party and for getting the groom home without mishaps after the revelry. Bachelor parties are notoriously raucous affairs and the groom is likely to wake up with a hangover at the very least. He is rarely expected to pay for anything himself.

The bachelorette party, or girls' night out, is organized by the maid of honor, who is responsible for the welfare of the bride. The celebration can take place in someone's house, or in a restaurant or club, and can take the form of anything from a lighthearted supper party to a bawdy visit to a local club. As with the groom, the bride is not expected to pay for herself.

The bride may wish to give a party for all the female members of the wedding party to thank them for being her attendants. It can be an intimate lunch, an informal afternoon tea, or an elegant dinner at a restaurant. Any bridesmaids who do not know each other can be introduced. Bridal showers are almost universal now. They are informal, female-only parties hosted by a close friend of the bride. Many hosts decide to have a particular theme for the occasion, and the idea is to "shower" the bride-to-be with thoughtful little presents.

BACHELOR PARTY

LOCATION

THOSE PRESENT

SPECIAL MEMORIES

BACHELORETTE PARTY

LOCATION

THOSE PRESENT

SPECIAL MEMORIES

BRIDAL SHOWER

LOCATION

THOSE PRESENT

SPECIAL MEMORIES

Ceremony Rehearsal

The official presiding over the ceremony may suggest having a rehearsal of the ceremony before the actual wedding day. Going through the ceremony procedure in precise detail will help everyone concerned understand exactly what is expected of them on the wedding day, and make them feel more confident. Even if you have attended many weddings as a guest, it is best to get specific instructions on what you have to do as a bride or groom.

DATE
....

TIME
....

THOSE PRESENT

Prewedding Dinner

Some families like to have a prewedding dinner. The evening before the wedding is an ideal time, when immediate members of both families and members of the wedding party can gather at the home of the bride's parents, at the hotel where out-of-town guests are staying, or in a favorite restaurant.

LOCATION
....

DATE
....

THOSE PRESENT

Chains do not hold a marriage together. It is threads, hundreds of tiny threads which sew people together through the years. That is what makes a marriage last.

SIMONE SIGNORET

Prewedding Jitters

You are making a huge commitment to another person when you get married, and no matter how much you love your intended, it is normal to feel anxious in the days leading up to the wedding. Being a bride or a groom can be a very stressful experience, planning a wedding is very demanding, and marriage is an enormous emotional undertaking.

Give yourself time to relax and unwind. Get regular exercise, treat yourself to a massage and a facial, and make sure you have a few quiet moments alone or with close friends. Try to arrange to be away from work for the week before the wedding day, to allow yourself ample time for last-minute preparations. The time off will also give you some much-needed time to yourself.

THE WEDDING DAY BEGINS

If everybody who is participating in the wedding—members of the wedding party, the caterers and staff, the photographer, the videographer, and the limousine company—knows what will happen when, it should help the day's proceedings run smoothly. Plan a detailed timetable and circulate a copy to everyone involved. Try to make the timetable as accurate as possible: check on the estimated length of the ceremony, allow for traffic when estimating the length of the trip between the ceremony and the reception, and give your guests adequate time to park. If there are any times on the schedule that are inflexible—for example, if you and the groom have to leave to catch a plane, or if the caterers have agreed to serve the food at a particular time—use these times as a starting point and fit everything else in around them. Follow the timetable, but don't panic if the schedule slips a little. Remember to relax and enjoy yourself.

BRIDAL PREPARATIONS   TIME

HAIRDRESSER

MAKEUP

BRIDE DRESSED

BRIDAL FLOWERS ARRIVE

PHOTOGRAPHY AT BRIDE'S HOME

TRANSPORTATION ARRIVES

DEPARTURES FOR THE CEREMONY   TIME

BEST MAN AND GROOM LEAVE

GROOM'S PARENTS LEAVE

BRIDE'S MOTHER AND ATTENDANTS LEAVE

BRIDE AND FATHER LEAVE

THE CEREMONY

BEST MAN AND GROOM ARRIVE

USHERS ARRIVE

GUESTS SEATED

PARENTS OF THE GROOM ARRIVE

BRIDE'S MOTHER AND ATTENDANTS ARRIVE

BRIDE AND FATHER ARRIVE

PREPARATIONS

CEREMONY STARTS

CEREMONY ENDS

PHOTOGRAPHS TAKEN

BRIDE AND GROOM LEAVE FOR RECEPTION

WEDDING PARTY LEAVES FOR RECEPTION

Blest is the bride on whom the sun doth shine.

ROBERT HERRICK, *A NUPTIAL SONG*

THE RECEPTION   TIME

ENTERTAINMENT BEGINS

BRIDE AND GROOM ARRIVE

WEDDING PARTY ARRIVES

GUESTS ARRIVE

RECEIVING LINE BEGINS

DRINKS SERVED

CANAPÉS SERVED

GUESTS SEATED FOR MEAL

FIRST DANCE

SECOND DANCE

FOOD SERVED

PHOTOGRAPH OF THE BRIDE

CHAMPAGNE TOAST

OTHER TOASTS

CUTTING THE CAKE

CAKE SERVED

BRIDE AND GROOM CHANGE CLOTHES

BRIDE THROWS BOUQUET

BRIDE AND GROOM LEAVE

GUESTS BEGIN TO LEAVE

THE CEREMONY

Finally, the long-awaited day has arrived. Today you are a bride and a groom about to make a public declaration of your love for each other. A marriage ceremony is deeply moving, and it formally unites you as husband and wife. You will remember these moments forever.

THE PLACE

....

DESCRIPTION

....

DESCRIPTION OF GROUNDS

....

SPECIAL FEATURES

....

WHY THIS LOCATION WAS CHOSEN

....

DENOMINATION

....

NAME OF OFFICIAL

....

Wedding Superstitions

The bride and groom should not meet on the morning before their wedding, and so they customarily spend the night apart.

The Bride
If the bride finds a spider in the folds of the wedding dress, or sees a lamb, a black cat, a toad, a dove, or a chimney sweep on the way to the wedding, that is thought to be a lucky omen.

The bride risks these bad omens: hearing a rooster crow after dawn, breaking a mirror on her wedding morning, or seeing either a funeral procession or a pig on the way to the wedding.

Nobody should see the bride wearing her full wedding attire before the ceremony. She should not even see herself fully dressed in a mirror, or try on the whole outfit together before the wedding day.

Some brides believe the dress should not be finished before the day, and will leave a few stitches to be completed on the morning of the wedding.

The bride must not cry before the ceremony, but can weep as much as she likes afterward.

The Groom
Once the groom has set out for the ceremony, he must not turn back under any circumstances.

He should pay the official an odd sum of money.

He should carry a good-luck charm in his pocket.

Seating Arrangements

The bride's family and friends sit on the left. The groom's family and friends sit on the right.

THE BRIDE'S FAMILY

FIRST PEW

SECOND PEW

THIRD PEW

THE GROOM'S FAMILY

FIRST PEW

SECOND PEW

THIRD PEW

Hail wedded love, mysterious law, true source
Of human offspring, sole propriety
In Paradise of all things common else.

JOHN MILTON, *PARADISE LOST*

THE SERVICE

MUSIC PLAYED BEFORE THE CEREMONY

THE WEDDING CERTIFICATE

NAMES OF WITNESSES

MUSIC PLAYED FOR THE PROCESSION
(THE BRIDE'S ENTRANCE)

REASON CHOSEN

THE MARRIAGE CEREMONY

RECORD OF YOUR WEDDING VOWS

GROOM

MUSIC PLAYED DURING THE RECESSIONAL
(AS THE BRIDAL PARTY LEAVES THE CHURCH)

OTHER MUSIC

BRIDE

(Remember you may add meaningful hymns or songs
throughout the service. The official performing the ceremony
may wish to deliver a brief sermon during the ceremony, or the
dictates of your religion may call for other elements.)

DESCRIPTION OF THE RINGS

THE BRIDE'S RING

THE GROOM'S RING

PHOTOGRAPH
OR
COPY OF THE MARRIAGE CERTIFICATE
(FOLD CERTIFICATE)

Pure, as the charities above,
Rise the sweet sympathies of love;
And closer chords than those of life
Unite the husband to the wife.

JOHN LOGAN, *THE LOVERS*

Marriage is destiny,
made in heaven.

JOHN LYLY, *MOTHER BOMBIE*

Throwing rice and more

As the couple emerge from the ceremony, guests may shower them with confetti and rice or, in some traditions, small wrapped candies. The confetti is frequently in the shape of horseshoes and shoes, which symbolize good luck. At one time, shoes were also thrown at newlyweds. Rice scattered over the couple symbolizes a wish for their happiness and prosperity. In past times, guests threw corn, thought to bless the marriage with fertility. Check beforehand whether throwing rice is permitted after the wedding, because some places prohibit the practice; bird seed is often an ideal substitute.

THE RECEPTION

If you arrive at the reception a little before the guests, give yourself a moment to collect your thoughts after the ceremony and to admire the reception setting, the beautifully coordinated decorations, table settings, and flowers. You deserve to have a wonderful time at your wedding reception after all the months of planning and organizing. Now you can turn your attention to welcoming your guests and receiving their congratulations.

Welcoming the guests

A receiving line may be a very formal idea, but it has many advantages. It allows each guest to be introduced to all members of the wedding party, to be welcomed to the celebrations, and to offer their congratulations to you and your groom. It is advisable to go through the guest list a day or two beforehand with both sets of parents, so that you are all acquainted with the guests' names.

The bride and groom should keep a lookout for friends of theirs who do not know either set of parents, so that they too are greeted warmly. The receiving line may also include the bridesmaids, unless they are very young, but usually not the best man, since he is the last to leave the ceremony.

At an informal reception, the guests could be greeted by the bride and groom alone. (This arrangement avoids any complications that might arise as to who stands where, if any of the parents are divorced or have remarried.) Alternatively, shorten the reception line by letting the fathers mingle. Bridesmaids may also join the party immediately. Expect to spend about one minute greeting each guest, and allow at least an hour for most receiving lines. Drinks should be served to guests as they arrive. While they wait to be received, ask the guests to sign a guest book with their good wishes to create a unique keepsake.

Order for the Receiving Line

Informal	Formal
Mother of the bride	Mother of the bride
Father of the bride	Father of the groom
Mother of the groom	Mother of the groom
Father of the groom	Father of the bride
Bride	Bride
Groom	Groom
Maid or matron of honor	Maid or matron of honor
Other attendants	Bridesmaids

THE PLACE

DESCRIPTION

SPECIAL FEATURES

WHY THE HALL WAS CHOSEN

PHOTOGRAPH OF THE RECEPTION SITE

DESCRIPTION OF DECORATIONS

COLOR SCHEME

THE SEATING PLAN

If you are having a sit-down meal, a seating plan is well worth making. Although it can be complicated and time-consuming to work out, a little thought from you about which guests will appreciate meeting one another should ensure that everyone will enjoy lively conversations at their table. It is not prudent to mix different generations, unless they are acquainted, or those who have little in common. Seat people with shared interests or mutual friends together. To guide guests to their seats, use place cards. Write a guest's name and table number on each card, and arrange them on a table near the entrance. Guests pick up their cards as they enter, then use the card to locate their table. Alternatively, have helpers greet guests at the door and guide them to their assigned table. This method can get frantic at a large wedding, however. Remember to label tables with their numbers.

HEAD TABLE

| BRIDESMAIDS | GROOM'S FATHER | BRIDE'S MOTHER | GROOM | BRIDE | BRIDE'S FATHER | GROOM'S MOTHER | BEST MAN |

TABLE 1 ....

....

....

....

....

....

....

TABLE 2 ....

....

....

....

....

....

....

TABLE 3 ....

....

....

....

....

....

TABLE 4 ....

....

....

....

....

....

TABLE 5

....
....
....
....
....
....
....
....

TABLE 6

....
....
....
....
....
....
....
....

TABLE 7

....
....
....
....
....
....
....
....

TABLE 8

....
....
....
....
....
....
....
....

TABLE 9

....
....
....
....
....
....
....
....

TABLE 10

....
....
....
....
....
....
....
....

TABLE 11

....
....
....
....
....
....
....
....

TABLE 12

....
....
....
....
....
....
....
....

THE WEDDING BANQUET

You might feel too excited to eat, but your guests will most probably have acquired an appetite after sitting through the ceremony and will look forward to a feast of food and wine. Sharing a meal and giving hospitality is an important and symbolic part of the wedding, one which will enable every one of your guests to partake fully in the celebrations.

MENU
....

HORS D'OEUVRES
....

SALADS
....

MAIN COURSE
....

SIDE DISHES
....

DESSERTS
....

CAKE
....

GUESTS' COMMENTS ABOUT THE FOOD
....

YOUR COMMENTS ABOUT THE FOOD
....

YOUR FAVORITE DISH AT THE WEDDING
....

Eating is not merely a material pleasure. Eating well gives a spectacular joy to life
and contributes immensely to goodwill and happy companionship.

ELSA SCHIAPARELLI, *SHOCKING LIFE*

DRINKS SERVED

WHITE WINES

....

RED WINES

....

CHAMPAGNE

....

OTHERS

MENU OR PHOTOGRAPH

CHAMPAGNE LABEL

Some people like to give their guests little bags of Jordan
almonds as favors. Traditionally it is thought to be lucky to give
five almonds, which represent the following qualities:

one for health; two for wealth;
three for long life; four for fertility;
five for happiness.

WEDDING TOASTS AND SPEECHES

Toasts and speeches should be well thought out, entertaining, and witty, and should last no longer than five minutes or so. Guests at a wedding reception are among the most responsive a speaker will ever encounter—they are in celebratory mood, full of affection for the bride and groom, and have been generously wined and dined. They will laugh at almost anything, and, provided the speech is well constructed, it should be a memorable and enjoyable experience for the speaker.

Only a few toasts must be made: the best man toasts the couple and their new life together (caterers will refer to this as the champagne toast); and the groom toasts his new in-laws, and any other hosts of the wedding.

However carefully you plan the date of your wedding, there will be some people who are unable to attend, but who send you their love and best wishes. Preserve these special messages; they will grow even more precious to you as the years go by.

FAVORITE QUOTATIONS FROM SPEECHES

BEST MAN
....
....
....
....
....
OTHERS
....
....

MESSAGES FROM ABSENT FRIENDS
....
....
....
....
....
....
....
....
....
....
....
....

CUTTING THE CAKE

The wedding cake has been a symbol of good luck and fertility for centuries. In Roman times the bride ate a portion of a cake made from flour and water, making a wish that she and her new husband would never lack for the basics in life. Every wedding guest would then be given a piece of the cake. Today we celebrate with elaborate, multi-tiered cakes, but we still retain the custom of a slice of the cake being distributed to each guest so all may share in the good fortune of the happy couple.

Cutting the cake is one of the highlights of the reception. The groom puts his hand over the bride's to hold the knife, and together they make the first cut in the cake. The bride and groom then feed each other morsels of the cake. According to folklore, if the bridesmaids or unmarried female guests keep their slices of cake and put them under their pillows at night, they will dream of their future spouses.

DESCRIPTION OF THE CAKE

NUMBER OF TIERS

TYPE OF CAKE

DESCRIPTION OF ICING

DESCRIPTION OF DECORATIONS

PHOTOGRAPH OF BRIDE AND GROOM
CUTTING THE CAKE

AT THE RECEPTION AND AFTER

Entertainment

The bride and groom maintain a very romantic tradition by leading the first dance; this will always be "your song." The music at your reception should reflect your taste. It should also be suitable for dancing yet at a level quiet enough to permit conversation.

....

MUSICIANS

....

MUSIC

....

SONG FOR FIRST DANCE

....

WHY YOU CHOSE THE SONG

....

SPECIAL MOMENTS

....

Going Away

Traditionally, guests should stay at the reception until the bride and groom have departed. If you do not plan to make a formal exit, you should make sure that everyone is aware of this, particularly older guests who may consider it to be bad manners to leave before the newlyweds. At military weddings the bride and groom leave by passing through two lines of guests who cross swords to form an arch.

....

BRIDE'S GOING-AWAY OUTFIT

....

GROOM'S GOING-AWAY OUTFIT

....

Throwing the bouquet

Just before the bride leaves the reception, the bridesmaids and unmarried female guests assemble together in anticipation of the bride throwing her bouquet. As the bride makes her exit, she turns and tosses her bouquet into the waiting crowd, or she may decide to throw it over her shoulder—in tradition, whoever catches it will be the next to marry. Some brides perform this ritual right after the ceremony; some use a "throwing bouquet" so they can keep their own.

THE BOUQUET WAS CAUGHT BY

....

Going-away car

Your going-away car is likely to have been secretly decorated with shaving cream, old shoes, and tin cans. Members of the wedding party will have great fun doing this, so take it with good cheer, it only happens once!

....

DESCRIPTION OF VEHICLE

....

DECORATIONS

....

Treasured Memories

Your wedding day is at an end; no doubt you are exhausted, but ecstatically happy. There were so many special moments during the day, and so many people made touching comments, that you will want to record them to treasure for ever.

....

....

....

....

....

....

....

....

O' the sudden up they rise and dance;
Then sit again, and sigh, and glance;
Then dance again, and kiss;
Thus sev'ral ways the time did pass,
Till ev'ry woman wished her place,
And ev'ry man wished his.

SIR JOHN SUCKLING, *A WEDDING BALLAD*

THE WEDDING NIGHT

The wedding is over, and the guests have gone home. This is the most romantic night of your life, when you and the one you love are finally man and wife. The celebrations are over, and you can enjoy being alone at last.

It is a night you will remember always.

WHERE IT WAS SPENT

DESCRIPTION OF THE EVENING

SPECIAL MEMORIES

He is the half part of a blessed man
Left to be finished by such as she;
And she a fair divided excellence,
Whose fullness of perfection lies in him.
O, two such silver currents, when they join,
Do glorify the banks that bound them in!

WILLIAM SHAKESPEARE, *KING JOHN*

THE HONEYMOON

Traditionally the groom takes on the responsibility for organizing and paying for the honeymoon, keeping the destination a surprise from the bride until after the wedding celebrations. Some couples are happy to follow this custom; others prefer to plan the honeymoon together. With all the festivities over, you can relax and savor the romance of being together all day, every day.

DESTINATION

DATE OF DEPARTURE

TRAVEL ARRANGEMENTS

ACCOMMODATIONS

SPECIAL MEALS

SPECIAL ACTIVITIES

SPECIAL PLACES

MEMORABLE DAYS

DATE OF RETURN

What is love? 'tis nature's treasure,
  'Tis the storehouse of her joys;
'Tis the highest heaven of pleasure,
  'Tis a bliss which never cloys.

THOMAS CHATTERTON, *THE REVENGE*

Crossing the Threshold

On returning home after the wedding, it is customary for the groom to carry his bride over the threshold of their home. The practice dates from pagan times, when the bride was borne aloft into her new dwelling so as to avoid the evil spirits that, it was thought, gathered outside the entrance. It also ensured that the bride did not step into her home left foot first—a bad omen. For the groom to carry the bride over the threshold meant the newlyweds would be blessed with good fortune all their days together.

WEDDING GIFTS

These pages provide a permanent record of each gift you have received, and enable you to double-check that all the guests have been sent a thank-you letter.

SENDER	GIFT	THANK-YOU LETTER SENT

SENDER	GIFT	THANK-YOU LETTER SENT

SENDER   GIFT   THANK-YOU LETTER SENT

SENDER	GIFT	THANK-YOU LETTER SENT

SENDER   GIFT   THANK-YOU LETTER SENT

....

....

....

....

....

....

....

....

....

....

....

....

....

....

SENDER	GIFT	THANK-YOU LETTER SENT

AFTER THE HONEYMOON

There will be some people who have been so helpful and supportive in organizing your wedding that they deserve an immediate note of thanks as soon as you return from your honeymoon. The person who performed your wedding will also appreciate a letter. It is a thoughtful gesture to invite both sets of parents for thank-you dinners as soon as possible. You may prepare the dinner at your new home, or you might prefer to take them to dinner at their favorite restaurant. Whichever you choose, do everything you can to ensure a pleasant evening for these special people.

THANK-YOU DINNER FOR BRIDE'S PARENTS

....
DATE

....
PLACE

....

....
SPECIAL MEMORIES

SPECIAL THANK-YOU LETTERS

....
SENT TO BRIDE'S PARENTS

....
SENT TO GROOM'S PARENTS

....
SENT TO WEDDING OFFICIAL

THANK-YOU DINNER FOR GROOM'S PARENTS

....
DATE

....
PLACE

....

....
SPECIAL MEMORIES

Cherishing the Memories

If you wish to keep your wedding dress to pass on to future generations, it should be professionally preserved after the wedding. First the dress is cleaned thoroughly, and the fabric specially treated to prevent it from deteriorating with age, and then it is stored in a sealed box to keep it free from dust.

Preserving your wedding bouquet is a charming and romantic custom. You can press the flowers and frame them, a practice much favored by the Victorians, or you may have the whole bouquet dried and encased in glass. Some flowers such as lilies are difficult to press successfully, so enlist the help of an expert.

The top tier of the cake is traditionally preserved and used to celebrate the first wedding anniversary. Cover the top layer in freezer wrap, put it in a suitable container, and freeze until a few days before your anniversary. In ancient times burying the cake in the ground was thought to aid fertility.

The First Anniversary

Your first wedding anniversary is an important milestone. Traditional wisdom has it that the first year of marriage is the hardest. Both of you will have had to adapt to your new life together, but now you can look forward to many happy years ahead—laughing, loving, and living.

....

DATE OF FIRST ANNIVERSARY

....

HOW YOU CELEBRATED

....

SPECIAL MEMORIES

Wedding Anniversary Presents

The celebration of different wedding anniversaries with specific types of gifts has a long tradition. This list has been modified over the years to reflect contemporary tastes.

First	Cotton
Second	Paper
Third	Leather
Fourth	Flowers (or silk)
Fifth	Wooden
Sixth	Sugar (or iron)
Seventh	Wool (or copper)
Eighth	Bronze (or electrical appliances)
Ninth	Pottery (or willow)
Tenth	Tin (or aluminum)
15th	Crystal
20th	China
25th	Silver
30th	Pearl
40th	Ruby
50th	Gold
60th	Diamond

The only thing that can hallow marriage is love, and the only genuine marriage is that which is hallowed by love.

LEO TOLSTOY, *THE KREUTZER SONATA*

FINANCIAL RECORD

Maintaining a detailed financial record will help you keep within your budget and make sure that all suppliers are paid as and when agreed. It is easy to get carried away with grand ideas when planning a wedding, but decide on a budget and follow it closely. You can be extravagant with some items, and economize on others. For example, you could invest in plenty of beautiful flowers or an exquisite wedding cake, and do without the luxury of a white Rolls Royce to take you to the wedding ceremony.

❀ Denotes items traditionally paid for by the bride and her family
✿ Denotes items traditionally paid for by the groom and his family

FOR THE BRIDE	BUDGET	ACTUAL	PAID
❀ VEIL			
❀ HEADDRESS			
❀ DRESS			
❀ LINGERIE			
❀ SHOES			
❀ GOING-AWAY OUTFIT			
❀ GOING-AWAY HAT			
❀ HAIR			
❀ BEAUTY TREATMENTS			
OTHER			

FOR THE GROOM	BUDGET	ACTUAL	PAID
✿ SUIT			
✿ SHIRT AND TIE			
✿ SHOES			
✿ GOING-AWAY OUTFIT			
OTHER			

FOR THE BRIDESMAIDS	BUDGET	ACTUAL	PAID
❀ GIFTS FOR BRIDESMAIDS			
❀ DRESSES AND ACCESSORIES			
OTHER			

FOR OTHER ATTENDANTS	BUDGET	ACTUAL	PAID
✿ GIFTS FOR GROOMSMEN			
✿ RINGBEARER'S OUTFIT			

STATIONERY	BUDGET	ACTUAL	PAID
❀ INVITATIONS			
❀ BRIDE'S STATIONERY			
OTHER			

FLOWERS	BUDGET	ACTUAL	PAID
✿ BRIDE'S BOUQUET			
✿ BRIDE'S HAIR			
✿ BRIDESMAIDS' BOUQUETS			
✿ MOTHERS' CORSAGES			
✿ BOUTONNIERES			

	BUDGET	ACTUAL	PAID
❀ FOR CEREMONY			
❀ FOR RECEPTION			
OTHER			

CEREMONY DONATIONS

	BUDGET	ACTUAL	PAID
❀ TO OFFICIAL			
❀ TO CHURCH/SYNAGOGUE			
OTHER			

RECEPTION

	BUDGET	ACTUAL	PAID
❀ HALL			
❀ TENT			
❀ DECORATIONS			
❀ MUSIC			

CATERERS

	BUDGET	ACTUAL	PAID
❀ STAFF			
❀ FOOD			
❀ WINE			
❀ CHAMPAGNE			
❀ OTHER DRINKS			
❀ EQUIPMENT RENTAL			
❀ LINEN			
❀ WEDDING CAKE			
OTHER			

TRANSPORTATION

	BUDGET	ACTUAL	PAID
❀ BRIDE'S CAR			
❀ GROOM'S CAR			

	BUDGET	ACTUAL	PAID
❀ TO CEREMONY FOR BRIDESMAIDS			
❀ TO CEREMONY FOR BRIDE'S MOTHER			
❀ TO RECEPTION			
OTHER			

PHOTOGRAPHY

	BUDGET	ACTUAL	PAID
❀ PHOTOGRAPHER			
❀ EXTRA PRINTS			
❀ VIDEOGRAPHER			
OTHER			

HONEYMOON

	BUDGET	ACTUAL	PAID
❀ TRAVEL COSTS			
❀ ACCOMMODATIONS			
❀ TRAVEL INSURANCE			
OTHER			

MISCELLANEOUS

	BUDGET	ACTUAL	PAID
❀ ANNOUNCEMENT OF ENGAGEMENT			
❀ MARRIAGE LICENSE			
❀ BLOOD TEST FOR BRIDE			
❀ BLOOD TEST FOR GROOM			
❀ WEDDING INSURANCE			
❀ RING(S)			
❀ ACCOMMODATIONS FOR WEDDING NIGHT			
OTHER			

NAMES AND ADDRESSES

For easy reference, use this section to record the details of people you will contact frequently.

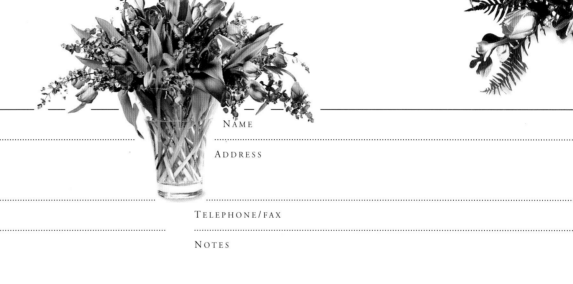

NAME

ADDRESS

TELEPHONE/FAX

NOTES

NAME

ADDRESS

TELEPHONE/FAX

NOTES

NAME

ADDRESS

TELEPHONE/FAX

NOTES

NAME

ADDRESS

TELEPHONE/FAX

NOTES

NAME

ADDRESS

TELEPHONE/FAX

NOTES

NAME

ADDRESS

TELEPHONE/FAX

NOTES

NAME

ADDRESS

TELEPHONE/FAX

NOTES

NAME

ADDRESS

TELEPHONE/FAX

NOTES

NAME

ADDRESS

TELEPHONE/FAX

NOTES

NAME

ADDRESS

TELEPHONE/FAX

NOTES

ACKNOWLEDGMENTS

Dorling Kindersley would like to thank the following for their kind assistance
in supplying items for special photography:
Maxine Ainscough; Arundel Photographic; Jerry Dalton; Finishing Touch;
Florians the Florist; Paul Goble Jewellery; Hanningtons Ltd.; Hatters;
Nicely Spliced; Trousseau of Nottingham Lace.

Photographs on pages 8 (center) and 50 (center) reproduced by courtesy of
Bridgeman Art Library, London.
Photographs on pages 2 (top left), 6 (bottom left), 28 (top right), 48 (bottom left),
49 (right), and 70 (center) reproduced by courtesy of Jane Packer from
Jane Packer's Flower Arranging (DK Publishing, 1995)